Introduction to *Daily Language Review*

P9-DJL-802

Why *Daily Language Review*?

The premise behind *Daily Language Review* is simple and straightforward—frequent, focused practice of a skill leads to mastery and retention of that skill.

What's in *Daily Language Review*?

The book is divided into 36 weekly sections. There are four practice items for each day of the week.

Monday through Thursday follow this format:

- sentences to edit—corrections need to be made in punctuation, capitalization, spelling, and grammar.

- items that practice a variety of language and reading skills.

Friday's practice involves a single job practicing a variety of skills, among them:

- categorizing objects
- reading for comprehension
- predicting outcomes
- sequencing
- unscrambling sentences
- combining sentences
- distinguishing between real and make believe
- alphabetical order
- writing and answering questions

An answer key for each week is provided on the same page as the Friday lesson.

Scope and sequence charts on pages 3 and 4 detail the specific skills practiced and show in which weeks the practice occurs. The skills chosen have been selected from a variety of language texts at this level.

How to Use *Daily Language Review*

There are several ways that the daily review practices can be presented. You may want to use all these presentations at times throughout the year to keep the practice fresh and interesting.

1. Make overhead transparencies of the lessons. Conduct the practice as an oral activity with the entire class. Write answers and make corrections using an erasable pen.

    Increased retention of the skills will occur if students mark the answers at the same time on a reproduced sheet or on the blank answer form provided on the inside back cover. As the class becomes more familiar with *Daily Language Review*, you may want students to mark their own answers first and then check responses by marking the items on the transparency.

2. Reproduce the pages for individuals or partners to work independently. Check answers as a group, using an overhead transparency to model the correct answers.

    Use these pages as independent practice only after much oral group experience with the lessons.

3. Occasionally you may want to use the lesson from one day or even a week as a test to see how individuals are progressing in their acquisition of skills.

    It should be stressed, however, that the greatest learning benefit will be gained from doing the practices orally so that students continually hear correct responses modeled by their classmates and the teacher.

Hints, Suggestions, and Options

1. Look ahead several weeks at the skills being practiced. If possible, teach new skills in formal lessons before asking students to practice these skills in the daily review.

2. Sometimes you will not have taught a given skill before it appears in a lesson. These items should then be done together, not independently. Tell the class that there is a skill they have not yet been taught. See if anyone knows the answer and wishes to explain it to the class. If not, use the review time to conduct a mini-lesson on that skill.

3. Customize the daily review lessons to the needs of your class.

•   If there are skills that are not included in the grade level expectancies of the particular program you teach, you may choose to skip those items—white them out or correct them before reproducing the page.

•   If you feel your class needs more practice than is provided, add these "extras" on your own in the form of a one-item warm up, a mini-post test, or ask students to provide another example.

Skills Scope & Sequence

	Reading Comprehension						Vocabulary & Word Study										Punctuation & Grammar								Reference
	Answering Questions	Categorizing	Inferring	Predicting	Real/Make-believe	Sequencing	Abbreviations	Comparatives	Compounds	Contractions	Homophones	Opposites	Plurals	Rhyming	Spelling	Word Families	Capitals	Commas	Identifying Sentences	Possessives	Pronouns	End Punctuation	Verb Tenses	Subject/Verb Agreement	Alphabetical Order
Week 1	X			X			X	X	X					X			X							X	
Week 2	X	X			X		X	X		X				X			X	X					X		
Week 3	X	X	X				X	X	X			X					X				X				
Week 4	X	X			X	X	X	X			X			X			X						X		X
Week 5	X	X	X		X		X	X	X				X				X	X					X		
Week 6		X	X				X	X		X			X			X							X		
Week 7		X	X				X	X	X				X				X								
Week 8	X	X	X	X			X	X		X					X					X					X
Week 9		X	X				X	X	X			X		X			X					X			
Week 10		X	X		X		X	X	X	X			X			X		X							
Week 11		X					X	X	X				X				X								
Week 12	X	X			X		X	X				X					X			X					X
Week 13		X			X		X	X	X				X					X							
Week 14		X	X				X	X		X				X				X							X
Week 15		X	X	X			X	X	X			X					X					X			
Week 16	X	X		X			X	X		X			X				X								X
Week 17	X		X	X			X	X	X				X					X							
Week 18	X	X	X	X			X	X		X		X	X		X			X							
Week 19	X	X	X				X	X	X				X					X							
Week 20	X	X	X	X			X	X		X				X	X			X			X				X
Week 21		X	X				X	X					X		X			X							
Week 22	X	X	X				X	X			X				X				X						
Week 23		X			X		X	X	X				X					X					X		
Week 24	X	X	X			X	X	X		X			X					X			X				X
Week 25		X		X			X	X	X				X					X							
Week 26		X	X				X	X		X			X				X						X		
Week 27		X					X	X	X			X						X			X				
Week 28	X	X					X	X					X					X							X
Week 29		X			X		X	X	X				X					X					X		
Week 30		X	X				X	X		X			X				X						X		
Week 31		X		X			X	X	X				X		X		X				X				
Week 32	X	X	X	X			X	X				X						X			X				X
Week 33		X			X		X	X	X				X					X			X	X			
Week 34	X	X	X	X			X	X		X					X		X								
Week 35		X		X			X	X				X						X	X		X		X		
Week 36	X	X	X	X			X	X				X					X				X				X

Sentence Editing Skills

Week	Sentence Beginning	I	Days, Months, Holidays	Books, Magazines	Proper Names & Titles	of People	Names of Places	Apostrophe in Contractions	Apostrophe in Possessives	Commas in Series	Periods in Abbreviations	Punctuation at End of Sentence	Comparative/Superlative	Adjectives	Double Negatives	Homophone Usage	Pronoun Usage	Subject/Verb Agreement	Word Order	Verb Usage	Spelling
Week 1	X	X	X				X					X									
Week 2	X			X								X									X
Week 3			X	X							X	X									X
Week 4	X	X			X		X					X									X
Week 5	X											X									X
Week 6	X											X									X
Week 7	X	X			X		X					X									X
Week 8	X				X		X					X									X
Week 9	X		X				X					X					X				X
Week 10			X				X			X		X									
Week 11	X		X									X									X
Week 12			X	X	X	X						X									
Week 13			X	X	X	X						X									
Week 14		X	X									X									
Week 15			X	X	X					X		X									
Week 16			X						X	X		X									
Week 17			X						X			X		X				X			
Week 18	X	X			X			X			X	X								X	
Week 19						X	X	X				X						X			
Week 20			X									X	X	X	X	X		X			X
Week 21	X	X								X		X		X			X			X	X
Week 22	X											X		X				X		X	X
Week 23			X	X	X					X	X	X		X						X	X
Week 24	X							X	X			X									X
Week 25			X			X	X		X	X		X		X				X		X	X
Week 26			X									X				X				X	X
Week 27	X		X						X	X		X		X	X					X	X
Week 28		X	X						X	X	X	X		X	X					X	X
Week 29	X								X	X		X	X	X		X				X	X
Week 30	X											X		X						X	X
Week 31											X	X			X						X
Week 32		X	X	X		X	X	X				X		X		X	X	X	X	X	X
Week 33									X	X	X	X		X						X	X
Week 34		X	X		X	X	X	X				X				X	X			X	X
Week 35	X	X	X			X	X		X	X		X		X	X	X	X			X	X
Week 36		X	X						X	X		X		X	X					X	X

Daily Language Review Grade 1 EMC 579

Monday ☆ 1

Find the sentence. Circle it.

1. The dog is barking.   Fuzzy the cat.

Which word is spelled correctly?

2. bok   book   buk   bouk

Make two words in the -an family.

3. _____ an   _____ an

Write your first and last name.

4. _____

☆ ☆ ☆

Tuesday ☆ 1

Finish the sentences.

1. The _____ squeaks.

2. The _____ purrs.

3. The _____ barks.

| dog |
| mouse |
| cat |

Fix the sentence.

4. i ride the bus

_____

Wednesday ⭐1

Fix the sentence.

1. my dad lives in new york

_____

Could it be true?

2. The hen walked on the road.   yes   no

3. The pen walked on the road.   yes   no

4. The men walked on the road.   yes   no

⭐ ⭐ ⭐

Thursday ⭐1

Choose the best word.

1. Mr. Black is tall. _____ can reach the top.   (Him   He)

2. Dr. Smith is short. _____ can't reach the top. (She   Her)

Find the words that rhyme with bell.

3. shell   well   tell   yellow

Fix the sentence.

4. i go to dance last saturday.

_____

Name: _____

Friday

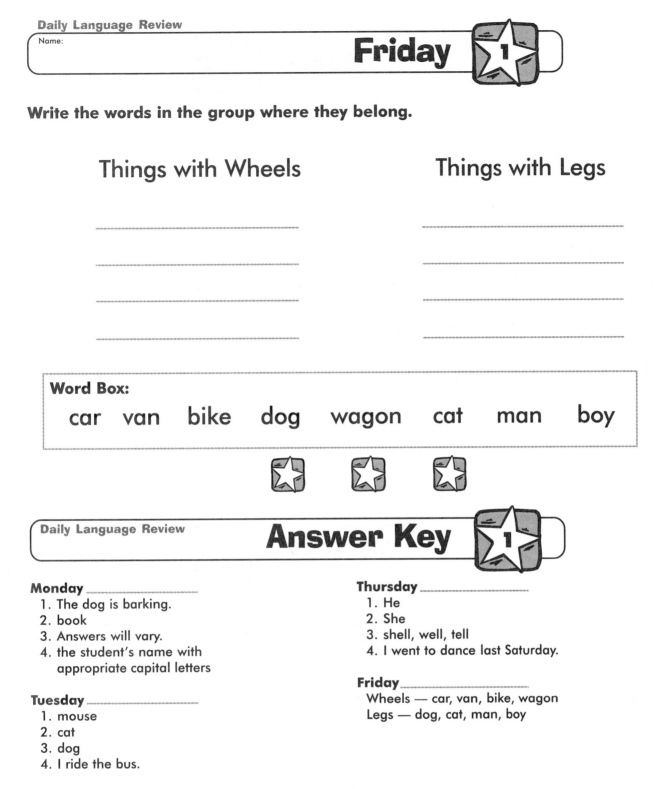

Write the words in the group where they belong.

Things with Wheels

_____

_____

_____

_____

Things with Legs

_____

_____

_____

_____

Word Box:

car   van   bike   dog   wagon   cat   man   boy

Daily Language Review

Answer Key

Monday
1. The dog is barking.
2. book
3. Answers will vary.
4. the student's name with appropriate capital letters

Tuesday
1. mouse
2. cat
3. dog
4. I ride the bus.

Wednesday
1. My dad lives in New York.
2. yes
3. no
4. yes

Thursday
1. He
2. She
3. shell, well, tell
4. I went to dance last Saturday.

Friday
Wheels — car, van, bike, wagon
Legs — dog, cat, man, boy

Name:

Monday ⭐2

Fix the sentence.

1. the ball is big and round

_____

Change the words to mean more than one.

2. ball _____

3. dog _____

4. boy _____

Name:

Tuesday ⭐2

Make two words that are part of the -ill family.

1. _____ ill   _____ ill

Fix the sentence.

2. mary is first in line

_____

Could it be real?

3. The mouse ate the cheese.   yes   no

4. The house ate the cheese.   yes   no

Wednesday 2

Which word is spelled correctly?

1. da   dae   day   dai

Give the two words for each contraction.

2. didn't _____   _____

3. it's _____   _____

Fix the sentence.

4. will you come too

⭐ ⭐ ⭐

Thursday 2

Fix the sentence.

1. she gave me a bok

Choose the best word.

2. The girls _____ the ball.   (kick   kicks)

3. Sammy _____ the cake.   (eat   eats)

What will happen next?

4. Milton gets in the car.

He goes to the store.   **OR**   He brushes his teeth.

Sue's birthday party will be October 1 at 3 o'clock at the skating rink. Help her fill out the invitation.

Come to my party!

Day _____

Time _____

Place _____

Sue

Daily Language Review

Answer Key 2

Monday
1. The ball is big and round.
2. balls
3. dogs
4. boys

Tuesday
1. Answers will vary.
2. Mary is first in line.
3. yes
4. no

Wednesday
1. day
2. did not
3. it is
4. Will you come too?

Thursday
1. She gave me a book.
2. kick
3. eats
4. He goes to the store.

Friday
Day   October 1
Time   3 o'clock
Place skating rink

Monday ⭐ 3

Find the words that rhyme.

1. ball   bug   fall

2. man   pan   mitt

Fix the sentence.

3. what a big dog

_____

Write the number.

4. two _____ four _____

⭐ ⭐ ⭐

Tuesday ⭐ 3

Tell whose it is.

1. It is the _____ kite.

2. It is the _____ hat.

Choose the best word.

3. I _____ a wasp in the bus.   (saw   seen)

Fix the sentence.

4. the teacher read to us

_____

Wednesday ⭐3

Tell what might happen.

1. The wind blew so....
   the flag waved. **OR** the train whistled.

2. The light turned red so...
   the cat meowed. **OR** the truck stopped.

Make two words in the -all family.

3. _____ all   _____ all

Fix the sentence.

4. my birthda is in august

Thursday ⭐3

Find the words that mean more than one.

1. cat   dogs   boy   girl   cars

Put these names in ABC order.

2. Max   Betty   David

_____   _____   _____

3. Sam   Tonja   Rick

_____   _____   _____

Fix this sentence.

4. we will sing with mrs black

Name:

Friday 3

Read the story.

Paul looked out the window.
He saw the street.
Two boys went by.
They had a bat and a ball.

Continue the story. Tell what you think the boys will do.

_____

_____

_____

Daily Language Review

Answer Key 3

Monday
1. ball, fall
2. man, pan
3. What a big dog!
4. 2, 4

Tuesday
1. girl's
2. boy's
3. saw
4. The teacher read to us.

Wednesday
1. the flag waved
2. the truck stopped.
3. Answers will vary.
4. My birthday is in August.

Thursday
1. dogs, cars
2. Betty, David, Max
3. Rick, Sam, Tonja
4. We will sing with Mrs. Black.

Friday
Answers will vary, but should reference the bat and the ball.
For example:

Pat grabbed his mitt. He ran after the boys to join the game.

Monday 4

Find the words that make a sentence.

1. She gave me a book. To the first grade.

2. The teacher read to us. Little Red Riding Hood and the wolf.

Which word is spelled correctly?

3. game   gaim   gam   gamm

Fix the sentence.

4. gia will win the game

Tuesday 4

Answer the questions.

1. Can a bird have a nest? _____

2. Can a bird have a house? _____

3. Can a bird have a truck? _____

Fix the sentence.

4. who came to your party

Wednesday 4

Give the opposites.

up big

1. down _____

2. little _____

Which word is spelled correctly?

3. werk   wirk   work   wrk

Fix the sentence.

4. tony and maria wrk hard

Thursday 4

Use me and I to finish the sentences.

1. _____ can read a book.

2. Sam gave the box to _____ .

3. My dad and _____ like to fish.

Fix the sentence.

4. i live in denver

Name:

Friday

Number the pictures in order.

Write or tell a story about what the pictures show.

Answer Key

Monday
1. She gave me a book.
2. The teacher read to us.
3. game
4. Gia will win the game.

Tuesday
1. yes
2. yes
3. no
4. Who came to your party?

Wednesday
1. up
2. big
3. work
4. Tony and Maria work hard.

Thursday
1. I
2. me
3. I
4. I live in Denver.

Friday
   2, 1, 3

Monday 5

Make two words in the -at family.

1. _____ at   _____ at

Find the name. Fix the capital.

2. ryan   boy

3. girl   rosa

Fix the sentence.

4. can you read the buk

Tuesday 5

Find the words that rhyme with dog.

1. log   dig   hog   frog

Answer the questions.

2. Can a fish work a VCR?   yes   no

3. Can a cat take a nap?   yes   no

Fix the sentence.

4. peter has a red hat

Wednesday 5

Which word is spelled correctly?

1. kum   cum   come   cahm

Choose the best word.

2. _____ went to the park.
   We   Us

3. Dad made _____ popcorn.
   we   us

Fix the sentence.

4. i go to scott elementary school

Thursday 5

Which word doesn't belong?

1. dog   cat   bird   mouse

2. grass   tree   rock   flower

3. star   house   sun   moon

Fix the sentence.

4. sam and bill went to see zack

Name: _____

Friday 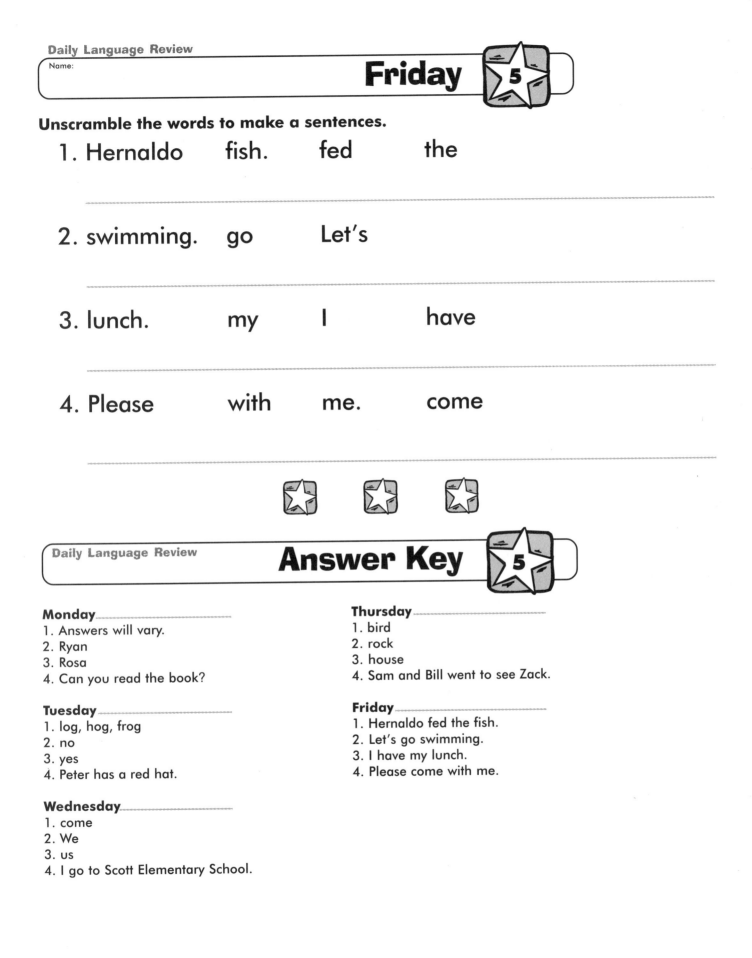 5

Unscramble the words to make a sentences.

1. Hernaldo   fish.   fed   the

_____

2. swimming.   go   Let's

_____

3. lunch.   my   I   have

_____

4. Please   with   me.   come

_____

Daily Language Review

Answer Key 5

Monday
1. Answers will vary.
2. Ryan
3. Rosa
4. Can you read the book?

Tuesday
1. log, hog, frog
2. no
3. yes
4. Peter has a red hat.

Wednesday
1. come
2. We
3. us
4. I go to Scott Elementary School.

Thursday
1. bird
2. rock
3. house
4. Sam and Bill went to see Zack.

Friday
1. Hernaldo fed the fish.
2. Let's go swimming.
3. I have my lunch.
4. Please come with me.

Name: _____

Monday ⭐ 6

Find the words that mean more than one.

1. lions   tigers   monkey   elephant

Give the two words for each contraction.

2. can't _____ and _____

3. don't _____ and _____

Fix the sentence.

4. did he open the door

Name: _____

Tuesday ⭐ 6

Make two words in the -ish family.

1. _____ ish   _____ ish

Real or make-believe?

2. Polly made a picture.   real   make-believe

3. Pat lives on the moon.   real   make-believe

Fix the sentence.

4. dad will kum to the party

Wednesday 6

Which word is spelled correctly?

1. with   witt   weeth   wiht

Choose the best word.

2. She_____ like to run.
   don't   doesn't

3. We_____ going home.
   was   were

Fix the sentence.

4. trudy can't go wth us

Thursday 6

What might happen next?

1. Gina plants a seed.
   The seed sprouts. **OR** Gina pets the cat.

2. The dog barks.
   Tom feeds the cat. **OR** Tom lets him in.

Answer the question.

3. Angelo only likes cuddly animals.
   Would Angelo like snails?   yes   no

Fix the sentence.

4. john hit the ball

Name: _____

Friday ⭐6

Which word tells about each animal?

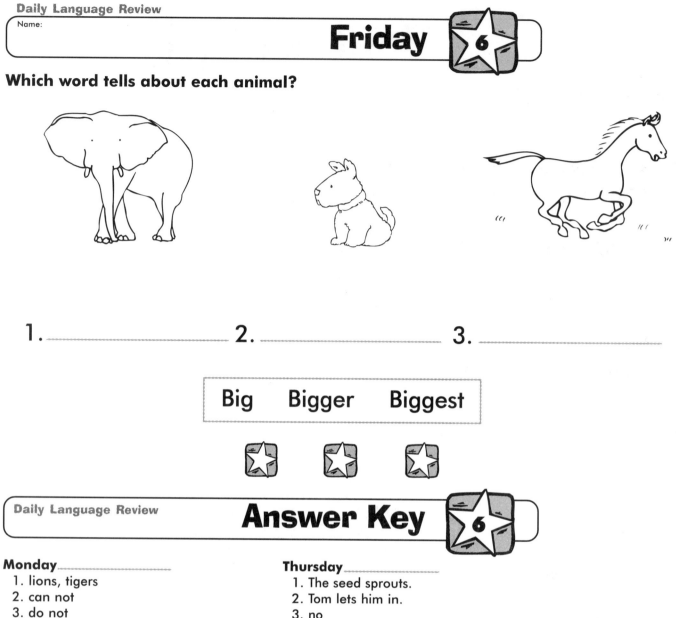

1. _____ 2. _____ 3. _____

| Big | Bigger | Biggest |

⭐ ⭐ ⭐

Answer Key ⭐6

Monday
1. lions, tigers
2. can not
3. do not
4. Did he open the door?

Tuesday
1. Answers will vary.
2. real
3. make-believe
4. Dad will come to the party.

Wednesday
1. with
2. doesn't
3. were
4. Trudy can't go with us.

Thursday
1. The seed sprouts.
2. Tom lets him in.
3. no
4. John hit the ball.

Friday
1. biggest
2. big
3. bigger

Monday 7

Make two words in the -ed family.

1. _____ ed   _____ ed

Read the sentence. Then fill in the blanks.

Mitten has white feet and black legs.

2. Mitten's feet are _____ .

3. Mitten's legs are _____ .

Fix the sentence.

4. little red riding hood had a basket

Tuesday 7

Find the words that rhyme.

1. hat   cat   car

2. fish   fat   wish

Choose the best word.

3. Lin will go _____ school.
               to   two

Fix the sentence.

4. when will fritz get here

Wednesday 7

Choose the best word.

1. We _____ down the hill.

    slided   slid

2. I _____ my bike to the store.

    rided   rode

Read the sentence. Tell when it happened.

3. Tom made a snowman.

    in the summer **OR** in the winter

Fix the sentence.

4. order the pizza from pizza hut

Thursday 7

Which word is spelled correctly?

1. pla   plai   pllaa   play

Fix the sentence.

2. <u>the little red hen</u> is a good bouk

What will happen next?

3. Jemma put on her pajamas. Then...

    she went outside to play. **OR** she hopped into bed.

4. The clouds looked black. Then...

    it started to rain. **OR** my brother smiled.

Name: _____

Friday ⭐ 7

Finish each sentence two ways.

It could really happen.

The bird _____ .

Yesterday the boy _____ .

It is make-believe.

The bird _____ .

Yesterday the boy _____ .

⭐ ⭐ ⭐

Daily Language Review

Answer Key ⭐ 7

Monday
1. Answers will vary.
2. white
3. black
4. Little Red Riding Hood had a basket.

Tuesday
1. hat, cat
2. fish, wish
3. to
4. When will Fritz get here?

Wednesday
1. slid
2. rode
3. in the winter
4. Order the pizza from Pizza Hut.

Thursday
1. play
2. The Little Red Hen is a good book.
3. she hopped into bed.
4. it started to rain.

Friday
Answers will vary.

Name: _____

Monday 8

Is it a sentence?

1. Chocolate chip cookies.   yes   no

2. Peter fed the fish.   yes   no

3. Cookie Monster loves cookies.   yes   no

Fix the sentence.

4. they have baby goats at the plum farm

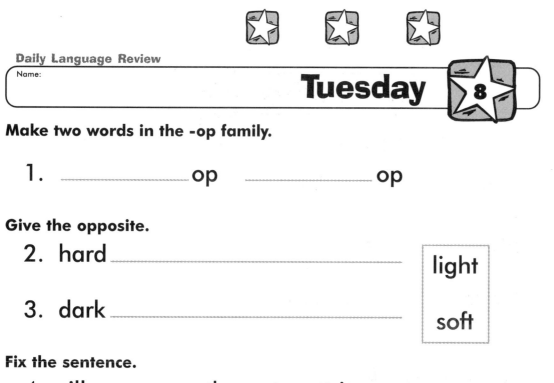

Name: _____

Tuesday 8

Make two words in the -op family.

1. _____ op   _____ op

Give the opposite.

2. hard _____

3. dark _____

light
soft

Fix the sentence.

4. will you cum wth me to get ice cream

Wednesday ⭐ 8

Which word is spelled correctly?

1. stahp   stop   stp   stob

Choose the best word.

2. Ms. Watson is a kindergarten teacher.

   _____ has a colorful room.   (She   He)

3. Mr. Gorze loves books.

   _____ always has one on his desk.   (She   He)

Fix the sentence.

4. peter pan lived in never-never land

Thursday ⭐ 8

Which name would come first in ABC order?

1. Bobby   Katie   Zander

2. Earl   Abdul   Mike

3. Sylvie   Nancy   Carmen

Fix the sentence.

4. next time goldilocks will knock

Number the sentences in order to tell the story.

Then draw a picture that shows what happened next.

☐ Pedro asked his grandma if he could go.

☐ Tomas called Pedro on the phone.

☐ He asked him to come play.

Monday
1. no
2. yes
3. yes
4. They have baby goats at the Plum Farm.

Tuesday
1. Answers will vary.
2. soft
3. light
4. Will you come with me to get ice cream?

Wednesday
1. stop
2. She
3. He
4. Peter Pan lived in Never-Never Land.

Thursday
1. Bobby
2. Abdul
3. Carmen
4. Next time Goldilocks will knock.

Friday
   3
   1
   2

Pictures will vary, but might show Pedro going out the door or the two boys playing together.

Make two words in the -it family.

1. _____ it   _____ it

Find the names. Fix the capitals.

2. town   dallas
3. u.s.a.   country

Fix the sentence.

4. i want to go to disneyland

Find the words that rhyme with fan.

1. ran   sand   man   pan   can

Choose the best word.

2. _____ want a cookie.
      me   I

3. Mr. Gerk and _____ worked together.
                me   I

Fix the sentence.

4. the box is from japan

Wednesday 9

Fix the sentence.

1. hannah and me went shopping

_____

Make a compound word.

2. side + walk = _____

3. class + room = _____

Answer the question.

4. Can a bird buy a car?   yes   no

Thursday 9

Fix the sentence.

1. are we there yet

_____

Is it a question?

2. What color is the dog   yes   no

3. How long will it take   yes   no

4. I want to go home   yes   no

Name:

Friday 9

Write the words in the group where they belong.

Things in the Sky

....

....

....

....

Things on the Ground

....

....

....

....

Word Box:

cloud   grass   house   bird   tree   tent   rainbow

Answer Key 9

Monday
1. Answers will vary.
2. Dallas
3. U.S.A.
4. I want to go to Disneyland.

Tuesday
1. ran, man, pan, can
2. I
3. I
4. The box is from Japan.

Wednesday
1. Hannah and I went shopping.
2. sidewalk
3. classroom
4. no

Thursday
1. Are we there yet?
2. yes
3. yes
4. no

Friday
Sky — cloud, bird, rainbow
Ground — grass, house, tree, tent

Name:

Monday ☆10

Make two words in the -ad family.

1. _____ ad _____ ad

Change the words to mean more than one.

2. one toy   three _____

3. one tree   two _____

Fix the sentence.

4. its a sunny dai

Name:

Tuesday ☆10

Give the two words for each contraction.

1. let's _____ and _____

2. don't _____ and _____

Which word is spelled correctly?

3. git   gett   gt   get

Fix the sentence.

4. its cold at the north pole

Wednesday  10

Read and decide.

1. The mouse carried the groceries into the house.   true   make-believe

2. The mouse nibbled the corn.   true   make-believe

3. The white mouse had pink eyes.   true   make-believe

Fix the sentence.

4. lets swim at the ymca

Thursday 10

Choose the best word.

1. The girls _____ read the book.
          has   have

2. Carlos _____ a red coat.
          has   have

What will happen?

3. Noah put milk on the cereal. Then....
          he gave it to his baby brother. **OR** he threw it in the trash.

Fix the sentence.

4. presidents' day is in february

Put the information into one sentence.

1. Chickens lay eggs.
   Turtles lay eggs.
   Stingrays lay eggs.

_____

2. I can make a shadow.
   A tree can make a shadow.
   The moon can make a shadow.

_____

Daily Language Review

Answer Key 10

Monday
1. Answers will vary.
2. toys
3. trees
4. It's a sunny day.

Tuesday
1. let us
2. do not
3. get
4. It's cold at the North Pole.

Wednesday
1. make-believe
2. true
3. true
4. Let's swim at the YMCA.

Thursday
1. have
2. has
3. he gave it to his baby brother
4. Presidents' Day is in February.

Friday
1. Chickens, turtles, and stingrays lay eggs.
2. A tree, the moon, and I can make shadows.

Monday 11

Make two words in the -up family.

1. _____ up _____ up

Find the words that rhyme with tent.

2. bent   cent   ten   sent

3. went   rent   spent   tenth

Fix the sentence.

4. grandma is coming for passover

Tuesday 11

Choose the best word.

1. _____ boys ran across the street.
   To   Two

2. I want a new book _____ .
   to   too

3. We went _____ the park.
   to   two

Fix the sentence.

4. we hide eggs for easter

Wednesday 11

Choose the best word.

1. Fred _____ his bat to school.
    brung   brought

2. Ellie _____ the ball off the tee.
    hitted   hit

Which word is spelled correctly?

3. tha   thay   they   thye

Fix the sentence.

4. i can rid a bike

Thursday 11

Find the letters that should be capitals.

1. eric hill wrote the book <u>where's spot?</u>.

2. at school we read <u>where the wild things are</u>.

What might happen?

3. Tony was invited to a birthday party. So...
    he bought a present. **OR** blew his nose.

Fix the sentence.

4. halloween is on friday

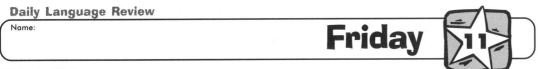

Friday 11

This is Yoko.

Use her name and 's to finish the labels.

_____ hands

_____ feet

_____ towel

_____ puppy

_____ bucket

Daily Language Review

Answer Key 11

Monday
1. Answers will vary.
2. bent, cent, sent
3. went, rent, spent
4. Grandma is coming for Passover.

Tuesday
1. Two
2. too
3. to
4. We hid eggs for Easter.

Wednesday
1. brought
2. hit
3. they
4. I can ride a bike.

Thursday
1. Eric Hill wrote the book <u>Where's Spot?</u>
2. At school we read <u>Where the Wild Things Are</u>.
3. he bought a present.
4. Halloween is on Friday.

Friday
Yoko's (Should be written on each of the 5 blanks.)

Name:

Monday 12

Tell if the words make a sentence.

1. The dog chased the cat.   yes   no

2. The bird. The nest. The egg.   yes   no

Make two words in the -eet family.

3. _____ eet   _____ eet

Fix the sentence.

4. monday morning i will go to school

Name:

Tuesday 12

Which word is spelled correctly?

1. lok   luk   look   louk

Read and decide.

2. Sam rode the alligator to school.   true   make-believe

3. Sam rode the tractor to school.   true   make-believe

Fix the sentence.

4. hop on pop is a rhyming book

Wednesday  12

Read and decide.

1. Sally is wet. She is wearing a special suit. Is she... taking a bath?   **OR**   swimming?

2. Todd sniffed. Then he chewed his bone. Is Todd... a dog?   **OR**   a bird?

Give the opposite.

3. go _____

Fix the sentence.

4. i have a baby sister named penny

Thursday 12

Choose the best word.

1. Mrs. Tripp likes to paint. _____ uses a big brush.

    Her   She

2. Mr. Jump likes to garden. _____ uses a little rake.

    He   Him

Write to tell which came first, next, last.

3. _____ Baby had babies.

    _____ Baby was a puppy.

    _____ Baby grew up.

Fix the sentence.

4. do you have vacation in july

Name: _____

Friday ⟨12⟩

Put the words in ABC order.

game   day   book   come   with

_____

_____

_____

_____

_____

⭐ ⭐ ⭐

Daily Language Review

Answer Key ⟨12⟩

Monday
1. yes
2. no
3. Answers will vary.
4. Monday morning I will go to school.

Tuesday
1. look
2. make-believe
3. make-believe
4. <u>Hop on Pop</u> is a rhyming book.

Wednesday
1. swimming
2. dog
3. stop
4. I have a baby sister named Penny.

Thursday
1. She
2. He
3. Last, first, next
4. Do you have vacation in July?

Friday
1. book, come, day, game, with

Monday  13

Write your teacher's name.

1. _____

Read and decide.

2. If the paint spilled, there would be a mess.   true   false

3. If it rained, the ground would be dry.   true   false

Fix the sentence.

4. i called my story "the laughing cow"

Tuesday 13

Read and decide.

1. The dog ate from a bowl.   real   make-believe

2. The dog drove a red car.   real   make-believe

Which word is spelled correctly?

3. boll   bol   ball   bal

Fix the sentence.

4. december is a cold month

Name: _____

Wednesday 13

Find the words that rhyme with dump.

1. bump   grump   dumb   lump

Choose the best word.

2. The table is big. Ten people can sit around _____ .

it   her

3. The mother cat is busy. _____ has four kittens.

She   He

Fix the sentence.

4. what will you eat on thanksgiving

Name: _____

Thursday 13

Put the words together to make a compound word.

1. sea + shell = _____

2. fire + truck = _____

Make two words in the -ail family.

3. _____ail   _____ail

Fix the sentence.

4. my brother is taller than steve

Name: _____

Friday ★13★

Write the words in the group where they belong.

Tall Things

_____

_____

_____

Short Things

_____

_____

_____

Word Box:

buildings ants trees sidewalks giraffes snails

Daily Language Review

Answer Key ★13★

Monday
1. name with appropriate capitals and title
2. true
3. false
4. I called my story "The Laughing Cow."
   Note: Do not hold students responsible for correct placement of period.

Tuesday
1. real
2. make-believe
3. ball
4. December is a cold month.

Wednesday
1. bump, grump, lump
2. it
3. She
4. What will you eat on Thanksgiving?

Thursday
1. seashell
2. firetruck
3. Answers will vary.
4. My brother is taller than Steve.

Friday
Tall — buildings, trees, giraffes
Short — ants, sidewalks, snails

Name:

Monday 14

Make two words in the -id family.

1. _____ id   _____ id

Give the word that means more than one.

2. one mouse   two _____

3. one goose   two _____

Fix the sentence.

4. i celebrate kwaanza

Name:

Tuesday 14

Give the two words for each contraction.

1. won't _____ and _____

2. doesn't _____ and _____

Which word is spelled correctly?

3. make   mak   maak   maik

Fix the sentence.

4. did you decorate a tree for christmas

Wednesday 14

Read and decide.

1. The mouse yelled, "Stop!" and ran away.   real   make-believe

2. The mouse squeaked and ran away.   real   make-believe

Fill in the blanks.

3. A _____ is bigger than a _____ .

Fix the sentence.

4. wednesday is in the middle of the week

Thursday 14

Choose the best word.

1. The boys _____ their favorite song.
    sing   sings

2. The girl _____ to the music.
    dance   dances

Read and decide.

3. Mabel eats grass and hay. She doesn't like her saddle.

    Mabel is a _____ .   (cow   horse   pig)

Fix the sentence.

4. my dad reads the sunday paper

Name:

Friday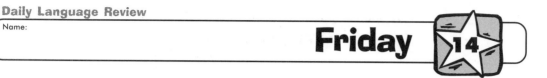

Read the story. Then draw or write to tell what might happen next.

It was a warm day.
Trudy and Sammy were playing in the yard.
A big cloud blew in.
It covered the sun.

Daily Language Review

Answer Key

Monday
1. Answers will vary.
2. mice
3. geese
4. I celebrate Kwaanza.

Tuesday
1. would not
2. does not
3. make
4. Did you decorate a tree for Christmas?

Wednesday
1. make-believe
2. real
3. Answers will vary.
4. Wednesday is in the middle of the week.

Thursday
1. sing
2. dances
3. horse
4. My dad reads the Sunday paper.

Friday
Reponses will vary. They should reflect the change in weather.

Name:

Monday 15

Make two words in the -ing family.

1. _____ ing   _____ ing

Find the capital letters. Circle them.

2. A   d   F   f   L   k   R   P   q   C

Find the words that rhyme with crab.

3. lab   tab   cab   crate

Fix the sentence.

4. last october i made a jack-o-lantern

Name:

Tuesday 15

Which word is spelled correctly?

1. fynd   find   feind   fid

2. tha   da   the   thea

Real or make-believe?

3. The elephant lost a shoe.   real   make-believe

The horse lost a shoe.   real   make-believe

Fix the sentence.

4. soccer practice is on tuesday and thursday

Name:

Wednesday 15

Choose the best word.

1. Mr. Brown read the book. _____ showed us the pictures too.

   He   Him

2. Mrs. Roberts threw the ball. _____ made a basket.

   She   Her

Answer the question.

3. Is an elephant small?   yes   no

Fix the sentence.

4. tashas party is on friday

Name:

Thursday 15

Make a compound word.

1. butter + fly = _____

2. in + side = _____

3. air + plane = _____

Fix the sentence.

4. i filled the dogs bowl

Friday ⟨15⟩

Write the words in the group where they belong.

Living Things

Non-living Things

_____

_____

_____

_____

_____

_____

Word Box:

car   tree   yo-yo   girl   dog   bell

Answer Key ⟨15⟩

Monday
1. Answers will vary.
2. A F L R P C
3. lab, tab, cab
4. Last October I made a Jack-o-lantern.

Tuesday
1. find
2. the
3. make-believe, real
4. Soccer practice is on Tuesday and Thursday.

Wednesday
1. He
2. She
3. no
4. Tasha's party is on Friday.

Thursday
1. butterfly
2. inside
3. airplane
4. I filled the dog's bowl.

Friday
Living – tree, girl, dog
Non-living – car, yo-yo, ball

Monday

Make two words for the -ake family.

1. _____ake   _____ake

Find the sentences.

2. We made cookies.   Good to eat.

3. Wagging its tail.   That puppy is cute.

Fix the sentence.

4. my dads car is blue

Tuesday 16

Which word is spelled correctly?

1. grein   gren   green   grn

2. bloo   bleu   blu   blue

Real or make-believe?

3. The car zoomed down the road.   real   make-believe

Fix the sentence.

4. luke didnt want to go

Wednesday  16

What will happen next?

1. Tom lost his new mittens. So...
   he put on a hat. **OR** he wore an old pair.

2. The alarm went off. So...
   Dad got up. **OR** John put on his pajamas.

Give the opposite.

3. night _____

Fix the sentence.

4. kennys coat is missing

Thursday 16

Choose the best word.

1. Sally and Tom ran home. _____ wanted a snack.

   They   Them

2. The cars waited. When the light changed, _____ left.

   they them

Which came first?

3. Rick baked the cake.   Rick sang Happy Birthday.

Fix the sentence.

4. wont you come with me

Friday 16

Mrs. Kehl's class has to go to lunch in ABC order. Make a list to help them get in order.

David	Appolonia	Chase	Heather
Barbie	Earl	Felice	Grant

1. _____

2. _____

3. _____

4. _____

5. _____

6. _____

7. _____

8. _____

Daily Language Review

Answer Key 16

Monday
1. Answers will vary.
2. We made cookies.
3. That puppy is cute.
4. My dad's car is blue.

Tuesday
1. green
2. blue
3. real
4. Luke didn't want to go.

Wednesday
1. he wore an old pair.
2. Dad got up.
3. day
4. Kenny's coat is missing.

Thursday
1. They
2. they
3. Rick baked the cake.
4. Won't you come with me?

Friday
Appolonia, Barbie, Chase, David,
Earl, Felice, Grant, Heather

Monday ⟩17⟩

Make two words in the -ent family.

1. _____ ent _____ ent

Find the words that need capital letters.

2. bambi   horse   mickey mouse   boy

3. home   washington   united states   farm

Fix the sentence.

4. miss browns key is on the table

Tuesday ⟩17⟩

Find the words that rhyme with boy.

1. toy   joy   Roy   bow

Which word is spelled correctly?

2. lik   like   lyke   lic

3. thes   thez   this   thisth

Fix the sentence.

4. tommy wants to see michael jordan

Wednesday 17

Real or make-believe?

1. The letter is in the mailbox.   real   make-believe

2. The lady is in the mailbox.   real   make-believe

Choose the best words.

3. _____ can go to the park.
   Me and you   You and I

Fix the sentence.

4. please hand me sharlas book

Thursday 17

Choose the best word.

1. Ms. White _____ my paper.
   taked   took

2. I _____ a robin.
   saw   seen

Give two words for the contraction.

3. isn't _____ and _____

Fix the sentence.

4. i and my dad mowed the lawn

Name: _____

Friday 17

Write a sentence to answer each question.

1. What do you like to eat?

_____

2. What is your favorite color?

_____

3. What will you do this weekend?

_____

4. Write your own question. Have someone tell you their answer.

_____

Answer Key 17

Monday
1. Answers will vary.
2. Bambi, Mickey Mouse
3. Washington, United States
4. Miss Brown's key is on the table.

Tuesday
1. toy, joy, Roy
2. like
3. this
4. Tommy wants to see Michael Jordan.

Wednesday
1. real
2. make-believe
3. You and I
4. Please hand me Sharla's book.

Thursday
1. took
2. saw
3. is not
4. My dad and I mowed the lawn.

Friday
Questions and answers will vary.

Choose the best word.

1. Bill and Sue _____ on the playground.

were   was

2. They _____ to play on the bars.

likes   like

Make two words for the -ub family.

3. _____ ub _____ ub

Fix the sentence.

4. tom gots a new toy car

Give the words that mean more than one.

1. one bird   three _____

2. one man   two _____

Real or make-believe?

3. The airplane flew in the sky.   real   make-believe

Fix the sentence.

4. the mail isnt here yet

Name: _____

Wednesday 18

Give two words for each contraction.

1. I'll _____ and _____

2. that's _____ and _____

What will happen?

3. Tomorrow is my birthday. So...
   I will have a party. **OR** I'll go to the dentist.

Fix the sentence.

4. mrs brown called on jose

Name: _____

Thursday 18

Which word is spelled correctly?

1. haf   hav   have   haav
2. girl   gerl   grl   gil

What does it mean? Draw to show.

3. Todd used the **bar** of soap.

Fix the sentence.

4. ill bring it to you

Name:

Friday  18

Read and decide.

The little bird flew up.
The little bird flew down.
The little bird looked for a good place.

The little bird has some string.
The little bird has some straw.
What is the little bird doing?

Daily Language Review

Answer Key 18

Monday
1. were
2. like
3. Answers will vary.
4. Tom has a new toy car.

Tuesday
1. birds
2. men
3. real
4. The mail isn't here yet.

Wednesday
1. I will
2. that is
3. I will have a party.
4. Mrs. Brown called on Jose.

Thursday
1. have
2. girl
3. picture should show a
   piece of soap
4. I'll bring it to you.

Friday
The little bird is making
a nest.

Name: _____

Monday 19

Make two words in the -ay family.

1. _____ ay _____ ay

Choose the best word.

2. I went to _____ house.

there   their

3. Put the pencil over _____ .

there   their

Fix the sentence.

4. thats a good book

Name: _____

Tuesday 19

Find the rhyming words.

1. will   Bill   doll   fill

2. hit   bit   kit   him

What will happen?

3. Mama cut the apple into little bits. Then...
   she made a pie. **OR** she went for a walk.

Fix the sentence.

4. will you please call donna for me

Name:

Wednesday 19

Whose is it?

Cari's <u>toy bunny</u> and Todd's <u>toy puppy</u> sat on the table.
1.   2.

Choose the best word.

3. He_____ a cookie.
      take   took

Fix the sentence.

4. me and my buddy play together

Name:

Thursday 19

Which word is spelled correctly?

1. duz   dus   does   doos

2. will   wil   wel   weel

Real or make-believe?

3. The tow truck pulled a mountain behind it.   real   make-believe

Fix the sentence.

4. come with i and see the birds

Read the address on the envelope. Fix the capitals.

mr. peter rabbit

2 mulberry lane

sussex, england

Daily Language Review

Answer Key **19**

Monday
1. Answers will vary.
2. their
3. there
4. That's a good book.

Tuesday
1. will, Bill, fill
2. hit, bit, kit
3. she made a pie.
4. Will you please call Donna for me?

Wednesday
1. Cari's
2. Todd's
3. took
4. My buddy and I play together.

Thursday
1. does
2. will
3. make-believe
4. Come with me and see the birds.

Friday
   Mr. Peter Rabbit
   2 Mulberry Lane
   Sussex, England

Name: _____

Monday   20

Make two words for the -ook family.

1. _____ ook _____ ook

Find the sentences.

2. Tommy lives in town.   In a very big house.

3. The best basketball player.   Kareem is on the team.

Fix the sentence.

4. me and my friends went to see <u>bambi</u>

Name: _____

Tuesday   20

Which word is spelled correctly?

1. tym   teim   time   tiem

2. tuday   todai   tooday   today

Real or make-believe?

3. The sky is falling.   real   make-believe

Fix the sentence.

4. nick and carmen isn't home yet

Name:

Wednesday  20

What will happen?

1. The little arrow pointed to the E. So...
   Dad put gas in the car. **OR** We stopped for an elephant.

2. I like to read <u>Jumanji</u> over and over. So...
   I hugged my dog. **OR** I checked it out of the library.

Give the opposite.

3. come ———————————————————————

Fix the sentence.

4. he sung a good song

Name:

Thursday 20

Which name would come first in ABC order?

1. Mandy   Kayli   Sarah

2. Sven   Nick   Abe

Choose the best words.

3. ———————————————— can go to the park.
   Me and you   You and I

Fix the sentence.

4. the team wore there red hats

Name:

Friday

Number the pictures in order. Then tell about what happened.

Daily Language Review

Answer Key 20

Monday
1. Answers will vary.
2. Tommy lives in town.
3. Kareem is on the team.
4. My friends and I went to see <u>Bambi</u>.

Tuesday
1. time
2. today
3. make-believe
4. Nick and Carmen aren't home yet.

Wednesday
1. Dad put gas in the car.
2. I checked it out of the library.
3. go
4. He sang a good song.

Thursday
1. Kayli
2. Abe
3. You and I
4. The team wore their red hats.

Friday
2, 1, 3
Explanations will vary.

Name:

Monday 21

Make two words from the -ug family.

1. _____ ug   _____ ug

Find the words that need capital letters.

2. mrs.   mr.   ms.   o'clock   dr.

3. the   tom   them   tyler   to

Fix the sentence.

4. us want a bag of popcorn

Name:

Tuesday 21

Which word is spelled correctly?

1. about   abut   abot   abowt

2. frum   from   frm   frahm

Real or make-believe?

3. The Big Bad Wolf blew down the pig's house.
       real   make-believe

Fix the sentence.

4. i can do it more better

Wednesday 21

Choose the best word.

1. Ms. White blows _____ whistle when it's time to line up.

    her   his

2. Mr. Vaas rides _____ bike to school.

    her   his

Which one doesn't belong?

3. shoes   gloves   socks   boots

Fix the sentence.

4. i gots a letter frm granny

Thursday 21

Make a compound word.

1. some + thing = _____

2. note + book = _____

Choose the best word.

3. I don't have _____ money.

    no   any

Fix the sentence.

4. will patrice come to beths party

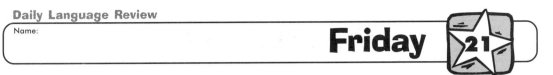
Sophia is a new girl at your school. Write three questions that you would like to ask her.

_____

_____

_____

_____

_____

Daily Language Review

Answer Key 21

Monday
1. Answers will vary.
2. Mrs., Mr., Ms., Dr.
3. Tom, Tyler
4. We want a bag of popcorn.

Tuesday
1. about
2. from
3. make-believe
4. I can do it better.

Wednesday
1. her
2. his
3. gloves
4. I got a letter from Granny.

Thursday
1. something
2. notebook
3. any
4. Will Patrice come to Beth's party?

Friday
Questions will vary.

Name: _____

Monday

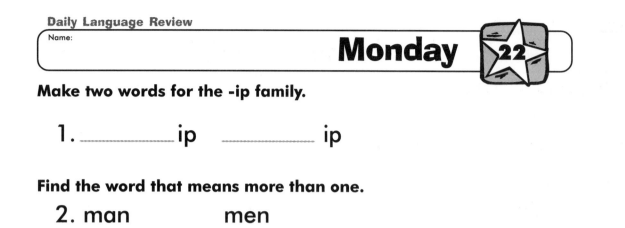

Make two words for the -ip family.

1. _____ ip   _____ ip

Find the word that means more than one.

2. man   men

3. people   person

Fix the sentence.

4. the girls has read the story about harry

Name: _____

Tuesday

Write the contraction.

1. you will = _____   '

2. you have = _____   '

Real or make-believe?

3. The bear stood on its hind legs.   real   make-believe

Fix the sentence.

4. he sung a good song

Name:

Wednesday 22

Which word is spelled correctly?

1. schul   schol   skool   school
2. went   wint   whent   wnt

What will happen next?

3. Mom gave Elise a quarter for helping with the wash. So...

Elise buried the quarter in the back yard.

OR

Elise put the quarter in her bank.

Fix the sentence.

4. youll need a hatt and mittens

Name:

Thursday 22

Choose the best word.

1. They_____ all going to Tina's house.

   was   were

2. Monty_____ staying at home.

   was   were

3. He's the _____ dad.

   best   bestest

Fix the sentence.

4. can you help the new grl wth hir buks

Name:

Friday

Read the clues. Tell which house each child lives in.

1.   2.    3.

☐ Brett loves to hear the water splash outside his window.

☐ Susie doesn't have to go outside to visit her neighbors.

☐ Ann and the third little pig in the story live in the same kind of house.

Answer Key

Monday
1. Answers will vary.
2. men
3. people
4. The girls have read the story about Harry.

Tuesday
1. you'll
2. you've
3. real
4. He sang a good song.

Wednesday
1. school
2. went
3. Elise put the quarter in her bank.
4. You'll need a hat and mittens.

Thursday
1. were
2. was
3. best
4. Can you help the new girl with her books?

Friday
Susie - 1
Ann - 2
Brett -3

Name: _____

Monday 23

Make two words for the -and family.

1. _____ and _____ and

Choose the best word.

2. Karen had _____ cookies.

                       four   for

3. She made them _____ Dennis.

                     four for

Fix the sentence.

4. youre my bestest friend

Name: _____

Tuesday 23

Find the rhyming words.

1. ball   bell   wall

2. room   zoo   zoom

Which word is spelled correctly?

3. hus   house   hows   howse

Fix the sentence.

4. please tell i all abowt your gaim

Wednesday 23

Finish the sentence to
answer the questions.

1. Whose bowl? It is the _____ .

2. Whose cat? It is the _____ .

3. Whose collar? It is the _____ .

Fix the sentence.

4. josie and i cant buy no candy

Thursday 23

Choose the best word.

1. I _____ a happy boy.

   drawed   drew

2. Sammy _____ fast.

   runned   ran

Which word is spelled correctly?

3. doun   dwn   down   dahwn

Fix the sentence.

4. we hav went to the park every saturday

Name:

Friday 23

Fix the note.

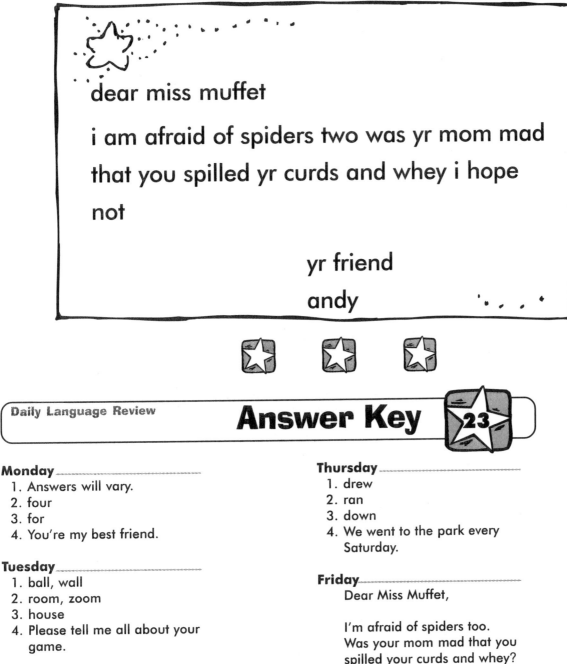

dear miss muffet

i am afraid of spiders two was yr mom mad that you spilled yr curds and whey i hope not

yr friend

andy

Answer Key 23

Monday
1. Answers will vary.
2. four
3. for
4. You're my best friend.

Tuesday
1. ball, wall
2. room, zoom
3. house
4. Please tell me all about your game.

Wednesday
1. cat's bowl
2. boy's cat
3. cat's collar
4. Josie and I can't buy any candy.

Thursday
1. drew
2. ran
3. down
4. We went to the park every Saturday.

Friday
Dear Miss Muffet,

I'm afraid of spiders too.
Was your mom mad that you spilled your curds and whey?
I hope not.

Your friend,
Andy

Name:

Monday 24

Find the sentences.

1. The leaves are falling down.   Red, yellow, and brown.

2. Cooking a batch of cookies.   Mom is busy.

Make two words in the -ig family.

3. _____ ig   _____ ig

Fix the sentence.

4. i runned faster than stevie and pete

Name:

Tuesday 24

Which word is spelled correctly?

1. wahnt   wnt   want   waant

2. sed   sayd   sayed   said

Real or make-believe?

3. The fish swam in a school.   real   make-believe

Fix the sentence.

4. wll you fynd the bawl i lost

Wednesday 24

What is happening?

1. Mom pins the pattern to the cloth. She cuts it out and sews it. Mom is making a dress. **OR** Mom is cleaning the house.

2. Bubba writes a note. He folds it up. He puts it in an envelope. Bubba is doing homework. **OR** Bubba is sending a letter.

Give the opposite.

3. short _____

Fix the sentence.

4. i rided my bike to marys house

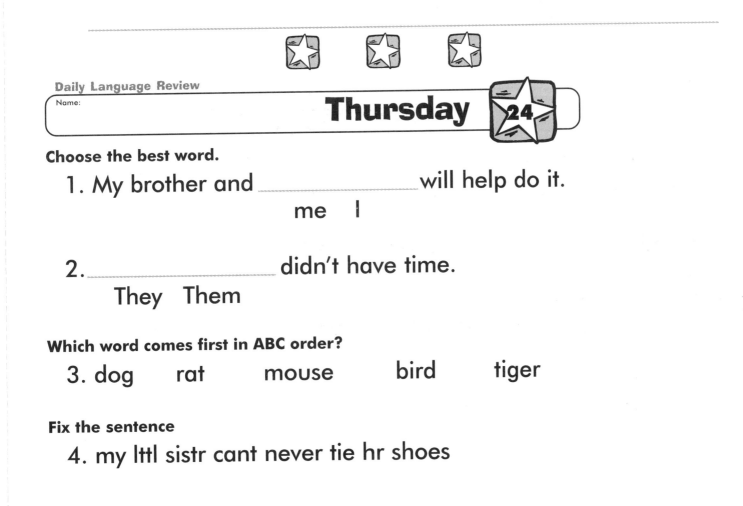

Thursday 24

Choose the best word.

1. My brother and _____ will help do it.

         me   I

2. _____ didn't have time.

    They Them

Which word comes first in ABC order?

3. dog   rat   mouse   bird   tiger

Fix the sentence

4. my lttl sistr cant never tie hr shoes

Name:

Friday 24

Put the sentences in order to tell a story.

☐ They went home happy.

☐ One day Little Bear went for a walk.

☐ They found some honey and ate it.

☐ He met one of his friends.

Answer Key 24

Monday
1. The leaves are falling down.
2. Mom is busy.
3. Answers will vary.
4. I ran faster than Stevie and Pete.

Tuesday
1. want
2. said
3. real
4. Will you find the ball I lost?

Wednesday
1. Mom is making a dress.
2. Bubba is sending a letter.
3. long
4. I rode my bike to Mary's house.

Thursday
1. I
2. They
3. bird
4. My little sister can't tie her shoes.

Friday
4
1
3
2

Name: _____

Monday ⭐ 25

Make two words for the -en family.

1. _____ en   _____ en

Which word is spelled correctly?

2. when   whin   whean   whn

3. suum   some   somme   sme

Fix the sentence.

4. he dont like tomatoes

Name: _____

Tuesday ⭐ 25

Find the words that rhyme.

1. cake   cook   bake   back

2. sun   sing   sink   wing

Real or make-Believe?

3. The duck quacked and swam away.   real   make-believe

Fix the sentence.

4. peter dont wnt to plai wth me

Wednesday ⭐25

Choose the best word.

1. Mr. Peters likes to fish. _____ always catches something.

    He   Him

2. Can you read the names? _____ are hard to see.

    They   Them

Which word doesn't belong?

3. tractor   barn   skyscraper   haystack

Fix the sentence.

4. du you lke mi gren dress

Thursday ⭐25

Make a compound word.

1. pan + cake = _____

2. base + ball = _____

Find the question. Circle it.

3. May I have some milk?   Two cookies with frosting?

Fix the sentence.

4. my mom wont leave me do it

Fix the list.

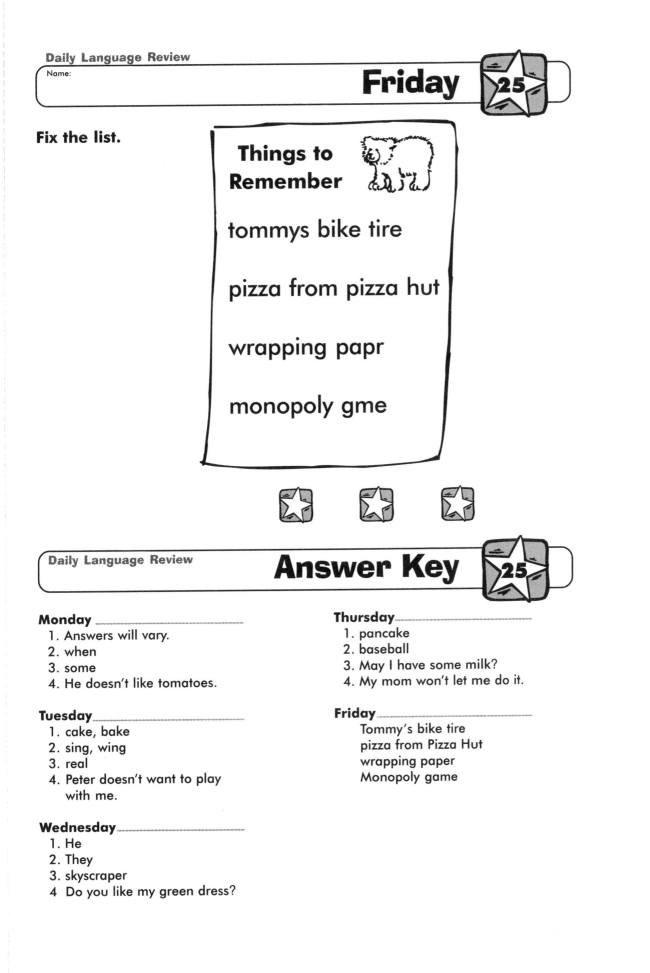

Things to Remember

tommys bike tire

pizza from pizza hut

wrapping papr

monopoly gme

Daily Language Review

Answer Key 25

Monday
1. Answers will vary.
2. when
3. some
4. He doesn't like tomatoes.

Tuesday
1. cake, bake
2. sing, wing
3. real
4. Peter doesn't want to play with me.

Wednesday
1. He
2. They
3. skyscraper
4 Do you like my green dress?

Thursday
1. pancake
2. baseball
3. May I have some milk?
4. My mom won't let me do it.

Friday
Tommy's bike tire
pizza from Pizza Hut
wrapping paper
Monopoly game

Name:

Monday 26

Write the word that means more than one.

1. one box   three _____

2. one lady   two _____

Make two words in the -og family.

3. _____ og   _____ og

Fix the sentence.

4. i dont have no money

_____

Name:

Tuesday 26

Write the contraction.

1. has + not = _____ '

2. have + not = _____ '

Which word is spelled correctly?

3. yer   yor   your   yr

Fix the sentence.

4. tony the tiger lks frosted flakes

_____

Wednesday 26

Choose the best word.

1. James _____ to ride the bus home.

   have   has

2. Doug and Colby _____ a computer at home.

   have   has

What will happen next?

3. Joe turned on the television. Then...

   he ran outside to play. **OR** he sat down to watch.

Fix the sentence.

4. pedro hasnt misst one dai

Thursday 26

Choose the best word.

1. A snail is _____ than a ladybug.

   bigger   biggest

2. My pillow is the _____ thing in my room.

   softer   softest

Yes or no?

3. The hamster lives in a cage.   yes   no

Fix the sentence.

4. fred brung his bat to schul

Name: _____

Friday 26

Which things would you need to bake a cake?

bowl	flour	tennis shoes	eggs
catcher's mitt	sugar	spoon	oven
cake pan	rake	recipe	mittens

Daily Language Review

Answer Key 26

Monday
1. boxes
2. ladies
3. Answers will vary.
4. I don't have any money.

Tuesday
1. hasn't
2. haven't
3. your
4. Tony the Tiger likes Frosted Flakes.

Wednesday
1. has
2. have
3. he sat down to watch.
4. Pedro hasn't missed one day.

Thursday
1. bigger
2. softest
3. yes
4. Fred brought his bat to school.

Friday
bowl, sugar, cake pan, flour, spoon, recipe, eggs, oven

Monday 27

Make two words in the -am family.

1. _____ am _____ am

Choose the best word.

2. Sammy _____ the book.
   red   read

3. The strawberries are bright _____.
   red   read

Fix the sentence.

4. my mom wont leave me do it

Tuesday 27

Find the rhyming words.

1. log   frog   lion   hog

2. sand   hand   band   fan

Choose the best word.

3. Ellie _____ the ball off the tee.
   hitted   hit

Fix the sentence.

4. its fun to ply at schul

Wednesday  27

Tell who it belongs to.

Mr. Black lives in a purple house. Mr. Brown lives in a white house.

1. Whose house is white? Mr. _____ is.

2. Whose house is purple? Mr. _____ is.

Real or make-believe?

3. When the princess kissed the frog, he turned into a prince.

real   make-believe

Fix the sentence.

4. we slided down the hill

Thursday 27

Which word is spelled correctly?

1. muther   moher   mather   mother

2. white   wheyet   wite   yiite

What is going on?

3. Mom squeezed the lemons and added sugar. Then she poured in water and stirred. Mom is...

making lemonade. **OR** fixing a salad.

Fix the sentence.

4. dad founded moms letter on the table

Name:

Friday 27

Betty wrote this poem for her mother. Fix the underlined words.

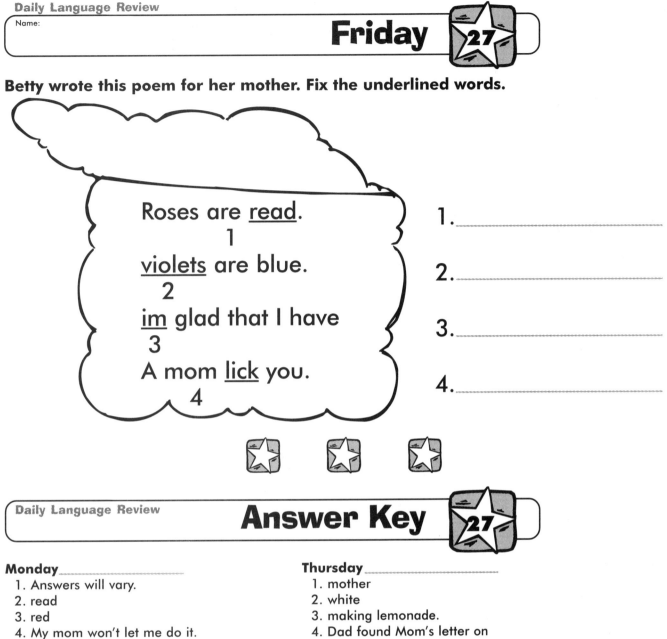

Roses are <u>read</u>.
    1
<u>violets</u> are blue.
    2
<u>im</u> glad that I have
  3
A mom <u>lick</u> you.
           4

1. _____

2. _____

3. _____

4. _____

Answer Key 27

Monday
1. Answers will vary.
2. read
3. red
4. My mom won't let me do it.

Tuesday
1. log, frog, hog
2. sand, hand, band
3. hit
4. It's fun to play at school.

Wednesday
1. Brown's
2. Black's
3. make-believe
4. We slid down the hill.

Thursday
1. mother
2. white
3. making lemonade.
4. Dad found Mom's letter on the table.

Friday
1. red
2. Violets
3. I'm
4. like

Name:

Monday 28

Which word is spelled correctly?

1. cud   cood   could   cude

2. fahther   fathur   father   fother

Make two words in the -ice family.

3. _____ ice _____ ice

Fix the sentence.

4. i have red yellow and blue paint

Name:

Tuesday 28

Find the sentences.

1. The little bird built a nest.   Standing on the branch.

2. Two little blue eggs.   The bird chirped happily.

Real or make-believe?

3. The cat climbed the tree trying to catch the bird.
              real   make-believe

Fix the sentence.

4. whin wil you go two seans house

Wednesday 28

What will you need?

For the baseball game

1. glove   hat   sled   skates   ball

For the bike hike

2. helmet   yo-yo   water bottle   bike   pump

Write the opposite.

3. black _____

Fix the sentence.

4. mrs tang made chocolate chip sugar and peanut butter cookies

_____

_____

Thursday 28

Choose the best word.

1. _____ dogs bark all the time.

   Them   Those

2. I want some of _____ cookies.

   them   those

Which comes first in ABC order?

3. red   blue   pink   yellow

Fix the sentence.

4. we took food water and a tent

Name:

Friday

28

Find all the words that tell where. Circle them.

The funny clown ran around the car.

First he got in it.

Then he got out.

He crawled over the car.

He even crawled under it.

Where could he be now?

Daily Language Review

Answer Key

28

Monday
1. could
2. father
3. Answers will vary.
4. I have red, yellow, and blue paint.

Tuesday
1. The little bird built a nest.
2. The bird chirped happily.
3. real
4. When will you go to Sean's house?

Wednesday
1. glove, hat, ball
2. helmet, water bottle, bike, pump
3. white
4. Mrs. Tang made chocolate chip, sugar, and peanut butter cookies.

Thursday
1. Those
2. those
3. blue
4. We took food, water, and a tent.

Friday
around, in, out, over, under

Name: _____

Monday 29

Make two words in the -aw family.

1. _____ aw _____ aw

Which word is spelled correctly?

2. lettle   litle   little   littl

3. whre   whare   wahre   where

Fix the sentence.

4. Abdul wont fnd nothing in the box

Name: _____

Tuesday 29

Fix the capitals.

1. sari, ann, and i went home.

2. bree, todd, and whitney rode to central park.

Find the rhyming words.

3. pen   hen   ten   tan   pin   men

Fix the sentence.

4. ann hided under the bed

Wednesday 29

Real or make-believe?

1. The men talked to the boys.   real   make-believe

2. The hen talked to the boys.   real   make-believe

Choose the best word.

3. _____ read a book last night.

   I   Me

Fix the sentence.

4. shes the most tall in our class

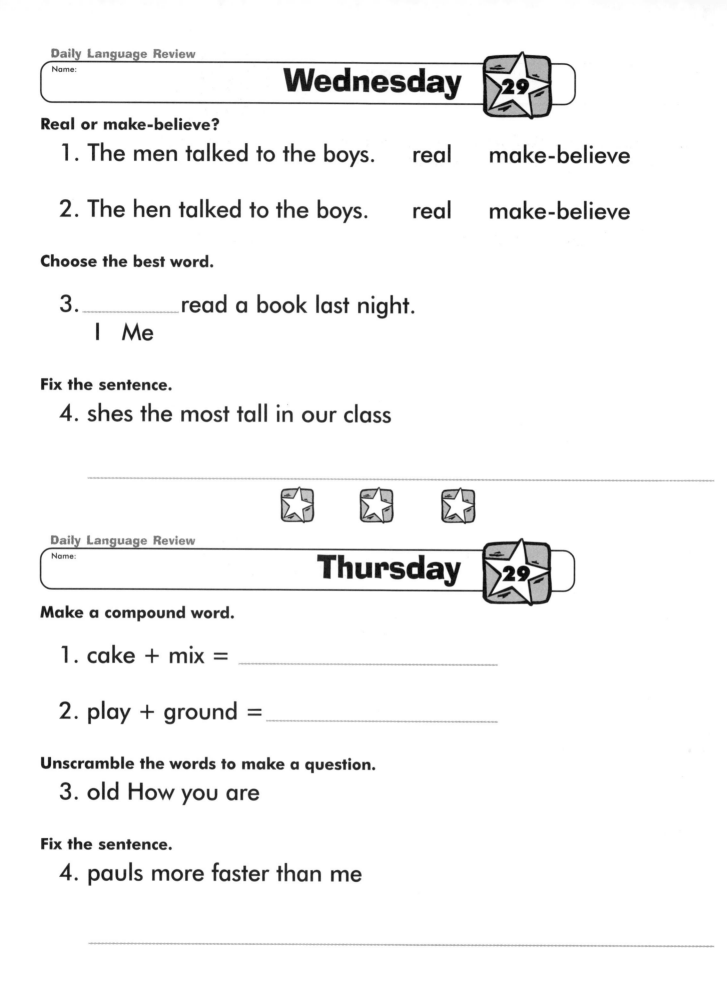

Thursday 29

Make a compound word.

1. cake + mix = _____

2. play + ground = _____

Unscramble the words to make a question.

3. old How you are

Fix the sentence.

4. pauls more faster than me

Some words sound alike, but they mean different things and have different spellings. Draw a picture to show what the two same-sound words mean.

Tom's plate is bare.	The bear had a cub.

Daily Language Review

Answer Key 29

Monday
1. Answers will vary.
2. little
3. where
4. Abdul won't find anything in the box.

Tuesday
1. Sari, Ann, and I went home.
2. Bree, Todd, and Whitney rode to Central Park.
3. pen, hen, ten, men
4. Ann hid under the bed.

Wednesday
1. real
2. make-believe
3. I
4. She's the tallest in our class.

Thursday
1. cakemix
2. playground
3. How old are you?
4. Paul's faster than me.

Friday
bare = empty   bear = animal

Name: _____

Monday 30

Write the contraction.

1. would + not = _____

2. could + not = _____

Make two words for the -ive family.

3. _____ive _____ive

Fix the sentence.

4. tha grl lived in tha gren huse

Name: _____

Tuesday 30

Find the word that means more than one.

1. hog   chickens   kitten   cattle

2. men   girl   boys   woman

Real or make-believe?

3. The paint dripped on the floor.   real   make-believe

Fix the sentence.

4. my litle sistr hitted the ball hard

Wednesday ⭐30

Which word is spelled correctly?

1. thenk   thinck   thnk   think

2. bahk   back   bck   baack

What will happen?

3. Ben put the kernels in the pot and plugged it in. Then he...
heard the baby cry. **OR** heard popping sounds.

Fix the sentence.

4. i aint gonna do that

Thursday ⭐30

Choose the best word.

1. Cherie _____ like peanut butter.
doesn't   don't

2. The boys _____ like pea soup.
doesn't   don't

Finish the word.

3. Your foot is long _____ than the baby's foot.

Fix the sentence.

4. my dog spot growed bigger

Name:

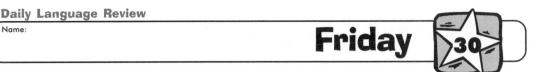

Friday 30

Andy wrote this note to Sam. Can you fix it?

sam,

meet me at south street

i hav sumthing special to show yu

andy

Answer Key 30

Monday
1. wouldn't
2. couldn't
3. Answers will vary.
4. The girl lived in the green house.

Tuesday
1. chickens, cattle
2. men, boys
3. real
4. My little sister hit the ball hard.

Wednesday
1. think
2. back
3. heard popping sounds.
4. I'm not going to do that.

Thursday
1. doesn't
2. don't
3. –er
4. My dog Spot grew bigger.

Friday
Sam,
Meet me at South Street.
I have something special to show you.
Andy

Find the rhyming words.

1. big   bug   rug   rub

Put in the commas.

2. Sunday May 1 1997

Make two words for the -et family.

3. _____ et _____ et

Fix the sentence.

4. wll you call mrs groom for me

Daily Language Review

Name:

Tuesday 31

Choose the best word.

1. Chad walked _____ the library.

          to   too

2. Billy's little brother wanted to come _____ .

                                two   too

What will happen?

3. Mom put sandwiches and fruit in a basket. She said we were ...
   going to have a picnic. **OR** going to clean the house.

Fix the sentence.

4. whre do you live

Name:

Wednesday 31

Choose the best word.

1. Yesterday I _____ to the zoo.

   went   goed

2. We _____ our bikes home.

   rided   rode

Finish the word.

3. Tom _____ shoe came untied.

Fix the sentence.

4. i lickt tha buk abowt tha duck named ping

Name:

Thursday 31

Which word is spelled correctly?

1. sah   saw   sahw   cah

2. over   oaver   ofer   ovr

Real or make-believe?

3. The dragon breathed fire and smoke.   real   make-believe

Fix the sentence.

4. dr seuss liked to write funny buks

Name:

Friday 31

Write the words in the group where they belong.

Soft Things

_____

_____

_____

Hard Things

_____

_____

_____

Word Box:

| pillow | rock | sidewalk | t-shirt | marble | fur |

Daily Language Review

Answer Key 31

Monday
1. bug, rug
2. Sunday, May 1, 1997
3. Answers will vary.
4. Will you call Mrs. Groom for me?

Tuesday
1. to
2. too
3. going to have a picnic.
4. Where do you live?

Wednesday
1. went
2. rode
3. –'s
4. I liked that book about the duck named Ping.

Thursday
1. saw
2. over
3. make-believe
4. Dr. Seuss liked to write funny books.

Friday
soft — pillow, t-shirt, fur
hard — rock, sidewalk, marble

Monday 32

Which word is spelled correctly?

1. hme   hoam   hom   home

2. took   tok   touk   tuk

Make two words in the -ick family.

3. _____ick   _____ick

Fix the sentence.

4. me and Chichi wants to plai at donnys house

Tuesday 32

Find the sentences.

1. Milly and the cute puppy.   He's so soft.
2. The water spilled.   Too many puddles in the yard.

Real or make-believe?

3. When she sprinkled magic dust on the pumpkin, it turned into a carriage.

                 real   make-believe

Fix the sentence.

4. cinderella weared a beautiful dress two the kings ball

Wednesday  32

Give the opposite.

1. front _____

2. to _____

What will happen?

3. Camille put on her new dress and brushed her hair. Her dad had promised to take her... to a concert. **OR** on a hike.

Fix the sentence.

4. which shoes should i wear to saturdays gaim

Thursday 32

Choose the best word.

1. _____wants to come with us.

   Her   She

2. I don't think Mother will let _____come.

        her   she

Which word comes first in ABC order?

3. Pluto   Donald   Mickey   Goofy

Fix the sentence.

4. i didnt see no mickey mouse at disneyland

Name:

Friday

32

Write 1, 2, and 3 by the pictures to tell their order.

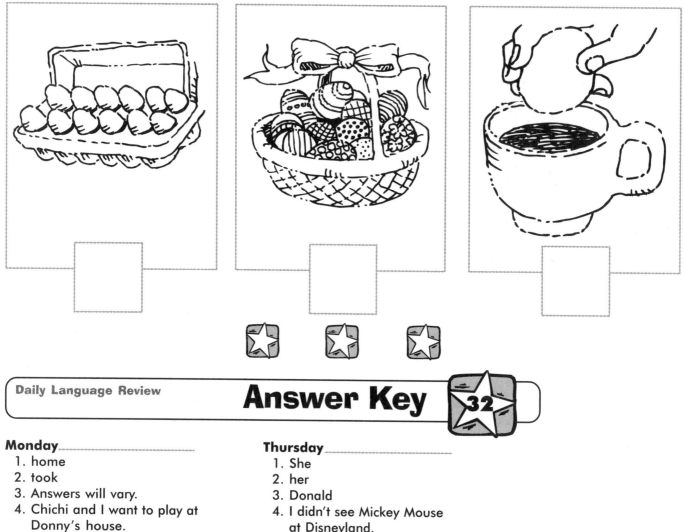

Daily Language Review

Answer Key

32

Monday
1. home
2. took
3. Answers will vary.
4. Chichi and I want to play at Donny's house.

Tuesday
1. He's so soft.
2. The water spilled.
3. make-believe
4. Cinderella wore a beautiful dress to the king's ball.

Wednesday
1. back
2. from
3. to a concert.
4. Which shoes should I wear to Saturday's game?

Thursday
1. She
2. her
3. Donald
4. I didn't see Mickey Mouse at Disneyland.

Friday
1   3   2

Choose the best word.

1. _____ can't reach the book.

   He   Him

2. Will you please help_____?

   he   him

Make two words in the -ap family.

3. _____ ap   _____ ap

Fix the sentence.

4. ron was afraid of bruces dog

Fix the capitals.

1. mr. felix smith
   301 glenmere blvd.
   evans, colorado

Find the rhyming words.

2. cake   cup   bake   rake

Put in the commas.

3. August 31 1976

Fix the sentence.

4. ms green wnts all the girls to taik tomorrows test

Wednesday 33

Which word is spelled correctly?

1. peeple   peaple   peopl   people

2. storee   stoary   story   storie

Real or make-believe?

3. The swimming pool was filled with lemonade.
        real   make-believe

Fix the sentence.

4. i need a hat a ball and mi bat

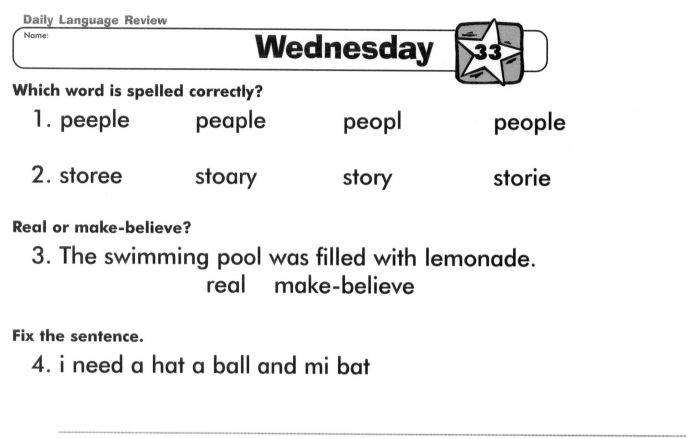

Thursday 33

Choose the best word

1. _____ dogs run fast.
   them   those

2. He broke_____ eggs.
        them those

Make a compound word.

3. mail + box = _____

Fix the sentence.

4. can patty and grace cum over to spend the nite

Write the words in the group where they belong.

Real People	Make-believe Characters
....	....
....	....
....	....
....	....

Word Box:

Peter Pan   Abraham Lincoln   Christopher Columbus   Superman
Dr. Seuss   Big Bad Wolf   Martin Luther King, Jr.   Pinocchio

---

Daily Language Review

Answer Key ⭐ 33

Monday
1. He
2. him
3. Answers will vary.
4. Ron was afraid of Bruce's dog.

Tuesday
1. Mr. Felix Smith
   301 Glenmere Blvd.
   Evans, Colorado
2. cake, bake, rake
3. August 31, 1976
4. Ms. Green wants all the girls to take tomorrow's test.

Wednesday
1. people
2. story
3. make-believe
4. I need a hat, a ball, and my bat.

Thursday
1. Those
2. those
3. mailbox
4. Can Patty and Grace come over to spend the night?

Friday
real — Dr. Seuss, Abraham Lincoln, Christopher Columbus, Martin Luther King, Jr.

make-believe — Peter Pan, Big Bad Wolf, Superman, Pinocchio

Monday 34

Choose the best word.

1. The boys _____ the balls at the target.

       throw   throws

2. The girls _____ the cargo net.

       climb   climbs

Fix the sentence.

3. tina and tasha rided to burger king

What will happen?

4. Scott put on his p.j.s and brushed his teeth. Next he...
   went out for a walk.   **OR**   jumped into bed.

Tuesday 34

Write the contraction.

1. that   +   is   =   _____ '

2. he   +   is   =   _____ '

Make two words in the -unk family.

3. _____ unk   _____ unk

Fix the sentence.

4. i will use dads paintbrush two paint the wall

Wednesday 34

Choose the best word.

1. There were three _____ in the cage.

      mouses   mice

2. The _____ flew in a giant V.

    gooses   geese

Real or make-believe?

3. The man balanced on the tight rope and walked across without falling.   real   make-believe

Fix the sentence.

4. toby and me are going to the big top circus

Thursday 34

Which word is spelled correctly?

1. weer   wher   were   wer

2. jiist   just   jst   jahst

Choose the best word.

3. Franco has the _____ chair in our classroom.

     bigger   biggest

Fix the sentence.

4. have you red the buk about peter rabbit

Name:

Friday

34

Read and decide.

I have a surprise in my hand.
It is small and white.
It has a long tail and whiskers.
It's name starts with an *m.*
What could it be?

Daily Language Review

Answer Key

34

Monday
1. throw
2. climb
3. Tina and Tasha rode to Burger King.
4. jumped into bed.

Tuesday
1. that's
2. he's
3. Answers will vary.
4. I will use Dad's paintbrush to paint the wall.

Wednesday
1. mice
2. geese
3. real
4. Toby and I are going to the Big Top Circus.

Thursday
1. were
2. just
3. biggest
4. Have you read the book about Peter Rabbit?

Friday
a mouse

Monday [35]

Choose the best word.

1. I _____ the answer to that question.

    know   no

2. There are _____ more apples on the tree.

    know   no

Make two words in the -ay family.

3. _____ ay _____ ay

Fix the sentence.

4. next year im not gonna go to no picnics

Tuesday [35]

Choose the best word.

1. Coach _____ me how to kick the ball.

    learned   taught

2. The boys _____ a mess with the paints.

    maked   made

Which word is spelled correctly?

3. woo   wu   whoou   who

Fix the sentence.

4. alice and me isnt going over their

Name:

Wednesday  35

Tell who it belongs to.

Lindy has a blue bike. Jean has a red bike.

1._____ bike is red.

2._____ bike is blue.

Read and decide.

3. Ms. Rupp put on her boots, her coat, and her umbrella. Is it...
   sunny? or stormy?

Fix the sentence.

4. she dont want to stawp at tims house

Name:

Thursday 35

Real or make-believe?

1. Tommy climbed up the tree and waved to me.
   real   make-believe

2. The turtle climbed up the tree and waved to me.
   real   make-believe

Find the rhyming words.

3. claw   clap   straw   draw   crawl

Fix the sentence.

4. next july im moving to california

Fix this note.

june 30 1998

dear grandpa

thank you for the new buk

its my favorite kind

i cant wait to read it

i love you

      frank

Daily Language Review

Answer Key 35

Monday
1. know
2. no
3. Answers will vary.
4. Next year I'm not going to go to any picnics.

Tuesday
1. taught
2. made
3. who
4. Alice and I aren't going over there.

Wednesday
1. Jean's
2. Lindy's
3. stormy
4. She doesn't want to stop at Tim's house.

Thursday
1. real
2. make-believe
3. claw, straw, draw
4. Next July I'm moving to California.

Friday
June 30, 1998

Dear Grandpa,
Thank you for the new book.
It's my favorite kind.
I can't wait to read it.
I love you.
Frank

Monday 36

Find the questions.

1. Can Sally come over?   Come soon?

2. Stop and go now?   Will Henry stop here?

Make two words in the -old family.

3. _____old _____old

Fix the sentence.

4. kelly touk the buk to lilys sister

Tuesday 36

Which word is spelled correctly?

1. vehry   viry   vry   very

2. smahl   smoll   small   smll

Real or make-believe?

3. The wolf blew down the house.   real   make-believe

Fix the sentence.

4. we runned around the block for times

Wednesday  36

What will happen?

1. Riley poured the hot tea over the ice cubes.

2. Rosa mixed the yellow and the blue paint.

Write the opposite.

3. under _____

Fix the sentence.

4. will you learn me how to swim on monday

Thursday 36

Choose the best word.

1. Colby and _____ went to the movie.

                I   me

2. Mr. Graham gave the paper to _____ .

                        I   me

Which word comes first in ABC order?

3. oranges   lemons   pineapple   grapefruit

Fix the sentence.

4. hes going to jims house

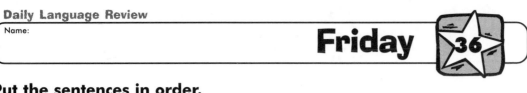
Put the sentences in order.

☐   The rain stopped and a rainbow appeared.

☐   The clouds got dark and it started to rain.

☐   The flowers smiled in the sunshine after their bath.

☐   Brecca enjoyed a wet walk under her umbrella.

Daily Language Review

Answer Key 36

Monday
1. Can Sally come over?
2. Will Henry stop here?
3. Answers will vary.
4. Kelly took the book to Lily's sister.

Tuesday
1. very
2. small
3. make-believe
4. We ran around the block four times.

Wednesday
1. The tea will get cold.
2. Rose will have green paint.
3. over
4. Will you teach me how to swim on Monday?

Thursday
1. I
2. me
3. grapefruit
4. He's going to Jim's house.

Friday
3
1
4
2